Transforming the Mind,
Healing the World

Marcia Rose

THE WIT LECTURES
HARVARD UNIVERSITY
THE DIVINITY SCHOOL

Jean Vanier (1993) *From Brokenness to Community*

Govindappa Venkataswamy (1994) *Illuminated Spirit*

Transforming the Mind, Healing the World

JOSEPH GOLDSTEIN

The Wit Lectures
Harvard University
The Divinity School

PAULIST PRESS
New York and Mahwah, N.J

Library of Congress Cataloging-in-Publication Data

Goldstein, Joseph, 1944-
    Transforming the mind, healing the world / by Joseph
Goldstein.
        p.   cm.—(Wit lectures)
    ISBN 0-8091-3484-5
    1. Spiritual life—Buddhism. I. Title. II. Series.
BQ5675.G657   1994
294.3'444—dc20   94-15319
                                                          CIP

Published by Paulist Press
997 Macarthur Boulevard
Mahwah, New Jersey 07430

Printed and bound in the United States of America

FOREWORD

*I*n this small book Joseph Goldstein conveys with clarity and concision some of the spiritual teachings, beliefs, values and practices we urgently need to help balance the materialism of our age—compassion, love, kindness, restraint, a skillful mind and a peaceful heart. Originally presented as the Wit Lectures at Harvard Divinity School, these essays clearly explain how to live a spiritual life. They reveal the need to combine faith with practice, freedom with responsibility and action with contemplation.

I, too, am firmly of the opinion that those who sincerely practice Buddha Dharma must also serve society. Too often we make what we call "the happiness of all sentient beings" the object of our prayers and meditations, yet when we rise from our meditation cushions we fail to give practical help to our neighbors and others in need. If we are to fulfill our altruistic wish, we cannot discriminate between spirituality and our life in society. Without the support of our fellow beings we could not practice at all, and without a concern for their welfare our practice has little meaning.

His Holiness
The Dalai Lama

INTRODUCTION

*I*n the midst of a secular society, it is often very difficult to support and sustain communities of faith and spiritual commitment. The Harold M. Wit Lectures at Harvard Divinity School were established in 1988 with that very challenge in mind. Harold Wit, Harvard College Class of 1949, stated his intention clearly and poignantly when he endowed a lectureship that would bring to the Harvard community "unusual individuals who radiate in their thought, word, and being those spiritual qualities and values that have been so inspiring and encouraging to me along my path. This in the hope that those listening to the lectures and being privileged to be in the good company of such persons might likewise be inspired and encouraged."

Joseph Goldstein fits that description admirably, for his life and his work exemplify a lived spirituality. In 1975 he helped to found the Insight Meditation Society (IMS), and today he is one of its primary guiding teachers. The Society's large residential retreat center in the rural town of Barre in central Massachusetts is dedicated to the practice and teaching of insight meditation *(vipassana)*, an ancient form of meditation originating over 2500 years ago with the teachings of the Buddha. The Society provides a secluded environment for intensive meditation throughout the year, and fosters an open community of spiritual participation and understanding enriched by the presence of Christians, Jews, Hindus, and those of many other traditions who come to deepen their wisdom. Mindfulness meditation cuts across all spiritual traditions, as Joseph Goldstein has said.

Vipassana is still a vital part of the Theravada Buddhist tradition. It is a simple, intensive, direct practice—the moment-to-moment investigation of the mind and the body through calm, focused awareness that slowly enables the mind to see into itself more clearly. Out of this balanced awareness and deepening insight, wisdom and compasssion emerge. Because compassionate action is the fruit of meditative practice, insight meditation also helps foster engaged spirituality and social concern—the practice of right action in a troubled world.

The Insight Meditation Society has a partner urban center, the Cambridge Insight Meditation Center, established in 1985. In 1989 Joseph Goldstein co-founded the Barre Center for Buddhist Studies. The Study Center is devoted to the consideration and investigation of the teachings of the Buddha, and to the integration of meditation practice with daily life. It contains a substantial library of Theravadin, Tibetan, and Zen Buddhist materials and offers a program of study developed in close conjunction with faculty from universities in the area, as well as with Buddhist monks, nuns, lay *dharma* teachers, scholars, psychologists, psychotherapists, and practitioners from various traditions.

Born in 1944, Joseph Goldstein graduated from Columbia University in 1965 with a degree in philosophy. He became interested in Buddhism and meditation during a stint with the Peace Corps in Thailand, where he taught English from 1965 to 1967. For the next seven years he practiced meditation intensively and studied in India under three teachers: Anagarika Sri Munindra, Sri S. N. Goenka, and Mrs. Nani Bala Barua (Dipa Ma). He returned to the United States and taught at the summer session of the Naropa Institute, the first American Buddhist college, in Boulder, Colorado. He began leading meditation retreats throughout the United States and different parts of the world. Since 1984 he has studied with the venerable Burmese meditation master, U Pandita Sayadaw. He is also the author of *The Experience of Insight: A Simple and Direct Guide to Buddhist Meditation* ([1976], 1983), *Insight*

Meditation: The Practice of Freedom (1993), and with Jack Kornfield, *Seeking the Heart of Wisdom: The Path of Insight Meditation* (1987).

In 1992 Joseph Goldstein delivered the Wit lectures published here to hundreds of people who filled two rooms at Harvard Divinity School, listening in perfect silence; we were in the midst of something quite extraordinary. In my experience it is rare to see such a continuity between silence and speech as we experienced with Joseph Goldstein. He was not just our speaker but also our teacher, and it is good to make available in print for the benefit of a wider audience his unusually clear, open, and practical reflections on the spiritual values of wisdom, compassion, and love.

Ronald F. Thiemann
Dean and John Lord O'Brian
   Professor of Divinity
Harvard Divinity School
Cambridge, Massachusetts

I

TRANSFORMING THE MIND, HEALING THE WORLD

I would like to speak about a triangle of three spiritual values—love, wisdom, and compassion—and how these key aspects of the spiritual life interrelate.

Dr. Irvin D. Yalom, a professor of psychiatry at Stanford University, wrote in his book *Love's Executioner* (1989):

I do not like to work with patients who are in love. Perhaps it is because of envy—I, too, crave enchantment. Perhaps it is because love and psychotherapy are fundamentally incompatible. The good therapist fights darkness and seeks illumination, while romantic love is sustained by mystery and crumbles upon inspection. I hate to be love's executioner.

Is there a kind of love that does not crumble upon inspection—that is actually compatible with illumination and enhances it? Is there a difference between that enchanted quality Yalom describes of falling in love, and a radiant quality of *living* in love?

I think that these two meanings of that overused word *love* are very different things. The Sanskrit word *maitri* and the Pali word *metta* both mean "lovingkindness" or "loving care." This is the kind of love I want to speak about here, a quality of friendliness, good will, generosity of the heart. When we are filled with lovingkindness and a sense of loving care, we feel a very simple wish: "May you be happy. May beings be happy. May all be happy." This quality of lovingkindness does not look for anything back. It does not give by way of a bargain. It does not say, "I will love you if you love me in return, or if you are a certain way." It is a love of caring, a love of kindness that does not seek any self-benefit; that is what defines its great generosity. Such love never associates with anything harmful, and that constitutes its great purity.

Let me tell you the story of someone who had an amazing capacity for this kind of *metta*, or loving feeling. Ryokan was an eighteenth and early nineteenth-century Japanese monk, hermit, and poet, a revered and much-loved figure to the Japanese even today. Ryokan lived alone in the mountains, and he would go off to play with children, to beg for his food, and otherwise to lead his spiritual life. One spring day, as it became warm and sunny, he picked the lice out of his monk's robes and put them on a rock to sun. But the really extraordinary thing was the fact that at the end of the day he picked the lice up and put them back on his robes. That is great lovingkindness.

This particular kind of love does not make distinctions among beings. It is very unlike love with desire or attachment, which we often confuse with *metta*. These two are really very different states. When you are feeling love mixed with desire, a common feeling in our lives, if you look carefully you will see that it is always love for a limited number of people. We may love and desire one person, or maybe two or three at a time, or maybe several in series. But I do not think there is anybody in this world who has desire for all beings. Universal caring lies outside the range of feeling love with desire. Lovingkindness, loving care, is so extraordinary precisely because it embraces all beings; it does not make distinctions.

The Practice of Love

We can develop this feeling within ourselves with a specific meditation practice whose progression is quite interesting. It starts with oneself. We extend loving feelings to ourselves. A surprising number of people find this practice difficult. This is one of the first insights that people get on a spiritual path, as they begin to look inside and see how much self-judgment, self-hatred, and unworthiness they feel. Very often a person has a hard time simply to direct loving feelings toward himself or herself: "May I be happy. May I be peaceful."

We move from loving ourselves to sending loving feelings to a great benefactor, then to loved ones, then to a neutral person, then to an enemy or a difficult person, and finally to all beings everywhere. We do all this in the solitude of meditation practice, but still it is not disconnected from how we are relating in the world.

I had a very interesting experience as I was doing this practice. My teacher told me that I was up to the stage of developing lovingkindness toward a neutral person, and he said to pick one. At first it was hard even to know what he meant by that. "Somebody whom you just do not really have much feeling about," he explained. I was in India at the time, and there was an old gardener at the little monastery where I was staying. I had seen him every day and had never really given any thought to him at all. He was just somebody I noticed in passing. It was quite shocking to me to see a whole category of people—a vast category of people—for whom I actually had no feeling. That in itself was a startling discovery.

I was visualizing and focusing on this old gardener all day every day for weeks, repeating over and over phrases like "May you be happy. May you be peaceful. May you be free from suffering." Then every time I saw him, my heart just opened, and I was in love with him. I reached a tremendous turning point, an understanding that how we feel about people, about situations, is up to us. It does not depend on the person. It does not depend on the situation. The person remained the same. He did not change what he was doing, or how he was relating to me. But because of a turn in my own understanding and practice, my heart began to fill with genuine feelings of care and kindness.

There is a very important lesson here about lovingkindness. When we develop this kind of love it does not depend on the other person. Because it does not depend on how the other person is, this love does not transform easily into ill will, into anger, or into irritation, as love with desire or attachment very often does. Rather, such unconditional love comes from our own generosity of feeling.

This power of lovingkindness and loving care has a tremendous strength, because there is nothing that falls outside its domain. That is why when we are with people who have developed this capacity to a very great extent—like the Dalai Lama, for example—we experience their tremendous kindness toward everyone. There are no exceptions. The Dalai Lama does not change how he feels when you are with him, and you can see that. You feel a state of blessing all the time. "Be happy": that is the wish of this particular feeling. We can develop it within ourselves. No one and no thing lies outside its field.

"In the cherry blossom's shade, there's no such thing as a stranger," wrote the sixteenth-century Japanese poet Issa. When I read this poem, I think, "That is lovingkindness." The feeling of lovingkindness, loving care, includes everybody.

We hear about this love, and we even recognize the purity and power of this feeling or state. The question is, how can we do it? Can we really develop this power in ourselves? It does not belong only to the Dalai Lama or Mother Teresa or some extraordinary being. The question for us is, can *we* do it? What is the wisdom that actually makes this inclusiveness possible?

Opening to Compassion

In the summer of 1989 a Harvard medical journal included an article about a Tibetan doctor named Tendzin Choedrak, who had been a personal physician to the Dalai Lama. In 1959 Dr. Choedrak was imprisoned by the Chinese and held by them for twenty-one years. As he described it, for seventeen of those next twenty-one years he was beaten and tortured daily, both physically and psychologically. His life was threatened daily. He described four points of understanding that made possible not only his survival, because people survive in very horrendous conditions in many ways, but also the great triumph of his heart. Astonishingly, Dr. Choedrak emerged from this twenty-one-year-long horror virtually free from signs of post-traumatic stress disorder. I think his story distills the wisdom we need to understand.

The first insight Dr. Choedrak had was to see his situation in a larger context. He saw his enemy as his teacher. The Dalai Lama often speaks of this understanding concerning Tibet and China. One's enemy teaches one patience. Dr. Choedrak felt that even in the most dreadful circumstances, in the most deplorable human situation, some human greatness was being accomplished. It takes an extraordinary perspective to see such a situation in the larger context of what human greatness can be accomplished. Can we see like this even in much less trying circumstances? Can we bring this perspective to our lives? Can we acquire this wisdom? Such vision makes possible the development and the strengthening of love.

Dr. Choedrak also understood that his enemies, his torturers, were human beings like himself. He did not forget the commonality of the human condition. The eastern notion of the law of *karma* means that actions have consequences, that actions bring results. Dr. Choedrak saw that these people who were being so cruel to him were actually in adverse circumstances just as he was. They were creating the *karma* that would bring their own future suffering. In seeing the common human condition in his situation, he let it be a source of compassion. This wisdom is very unusual, because often people use their understanding of the law of *karma* or retribution as a vehicle for revenge: "They will get theirs." Instead Dr. Choedrak saw *karma* as a vehicle for compassion. This is the wisdom we need to integrate into our lives: that we are all in the same situation.

Dr. Choedrak's third insight was the need to let go of pride and the feeling of self-importance. He actually attributed his survival to this ability to let go of self-righteousness. This insight is also a tremendous lesson in the spiritual journey, and it comes up again and again.

Years ago I was practicing meditation in India and faced much less trying circumstances than Dr. Choedrak faced, but circumstances that were trying enough. As the summer months came, it grew very hot on the plains, so I decided to go up to the Himalayas, rent a cottage, and continue my spiritual practice there. It was beautiful and quiet among the hill stations of the mountains in India. I settled into my routine of intensive practice.

Just below my cottage was a big, open field, and a few weeks after I arrived a group called the Delhi Girls came to it. The Delhi Girls were a kind of paramilitary Girl Scout troop. Not only did they set up camp, but they also set up loudspeakers. From six o'clock in the morning until ten o'clock at night, they played loud Hindi film music.

I watched my mind go through a tremendous range of emotions, from real anger, even rage, to a feeling of self-importance: "How can they do this to me? I came here to get enlightened!" It took quite a while for my mind to work through all of that, to let go of the feeling of self-importance and self-righteousness, and just to let things be. But when my mind finally settled down, it did let go in that way. Then the din of film music in the middle of a meditation retreat was no longer a problem.

The last of Dr. Choedrak's insights that allowed him to triumph in his situation was a principle that is common to many spiritual traditions: the understanding that hatred never eliminates hatred. Hatred, anger, and ill will never cease in response to hatred, anger, and ill will. They only cease in response to love. We need to remember and reflect on this wisdom, because it is just this wisdom that makes possible the feeling of love. Love grows when we see that there are no viable alternatives.

When we have developed a heart of generosity, a heart that wishes well to *all* beings, not just a few, then when we come close to suffering in the world, the heart moves to alleviate that suffering. Because of that foundation of good will, that foundation in us of *metta*, of lovingkindness, then we feel the impulse to do something about suffering. That impulse is compassion, the feeling that motivates us to act. Ryokan, that hermit monk who wrote such wonderful poetry, wrote, "Oh that my monk's robes were wide enough to gather up all the people in this floating world." What a wonderful image of compassion. Can we do that? Can we extend our compassion to that extent?

The willingness to come close to suffering opens us to compassion. Suffering is all around us. We do not have to look far. The nightly news programs are catalogs of suffering in the world. Can we be open to that? Can we actually relate to it, or has it all become too depersonalized?

We can also see suffering in our own bodies,

especially as we grow older. But it does not always wait. The nature of the body is to become sick, to fall ill, to feel pain, to suffer. If we really look, we also see the obvious, the huge amount of suffering going on in our minds—anger, hatred, fear, loneliness, anxiety, boredom…There are so many feelings, and they are all so prevalent in our culture and our society. Many of us have a fair degree of material comfort, yet when we look carefully at what is going on, our minds reflect the suffering that is really there. When we see suffering as an individual problem, whether our own or somebody else's, then we feel pity. Sometimes that feeling gets translated into self-pity or pity for another. When we understand suffering not as an individual problem, but as a universal experience, then this perception gives rise to the feeling of compassion. Then we experience, not a feeling of separation, but rather a feeling of oneness, a feeling that we all share in this universal predicament. That is what opens our hearts.

Unfortunately, often we are not open to the suffering. We do not like to feel it. We find ourselves closed off. We have been conditioned to avoid it and defend ourselves against it: "Let me not see the suffering. Let me not feel it." This avoidance becomes very obvious in meditation when we deal with physical pain. People who come to our meditation center in Barre, Massachusetts, often have this idea: "I will go on a retreat, I will sit there in bliss, and it will be a great spiritual high." They are in for a shocking awakening, because meditation is really about coming in touch with what is actually there. Especially at the beginning of the practice, many people need to get in touch with physical pain. In meditation practice it becomes so clear from very early on how conditioned our response to pain is. We do not like it. There is fear, there is self-pity, there is defensiveness, there is bargaining, there is pushing it away—"I'll watch you if you go away"—which is very different from opening up to it, allowing it, feeling it.

Our relationship to pain in the body tells us a lot about our relationship to pain in life. It is a very good measure of whether we are open or whether we are defensive. We can see how we also close off to certain emotions. As with physical pain, there are different emotions with which we are not comfortable: anger, sadness, fear, unworthiness, or many others. We do not like them. Think for a moment of what we do as a culture, as a society, in order not to feel boredom. It is astounding. People are so afraid of that feeling that they create whole lives so as not to feel it, a rush of activity, business, and work. Or think of the fear of feeling lonely. It is an unpleasant feeling if we are not willing to be with it, if we are not willing to explore that feeling in ourselves, to see that part of ourselves. Then we build whole structures in our lives to avoid feeling it.

Our conditioned reaction to any kind of unpleasantness is so strong that as soon as the unpleasantness comes, we close it off and avoid it, so we do not feel it. We just do not let unpleasant situations in. However, it is much simpler to feel these feelings than to try to avoid them. They do not last very long. They are there for a while, and we feel them, and they are unpleasant. But they go, and then something else comes.

Let me tell another story from my days of practicing meditation in India. I was living in a little hut, about six feet by seven feet. It had a canvas flap instead of a door. I was sitting on my bed meditating, and a cat wandered in and plopped down on my lap. I took the cat and tossed it out the door. Ten seconds later it was back on my lap. We got into a sort of dance, this cat and I. I would toss it out, and it would come back. I tossed it out because I was trying to meditate, to get enlightened. But the cat kept returning. I was getting more and more irritated, more and more annoyed with the persistence of the cat. Finally, after about a half-hour of this coming in and tossing out, I had to surrender. There was nothing else to do. There was no way to block off the door. I sat there, the cat came back in, and it got on my lap. But I did not do anything. I just let go. Thirty seconds later the cat got up and walked out. So you see, our teachers come in many forms.

We all need to learn. Sometimes it is a slow learning, and sometimes it is a little faster. But we need to learn how to open ourselves to what is difficult and painful, even in rather trivial instances like this one with the cat, because often there is a deep lesson in them. Sometimes we learn in very profound instances. But it is only by a willingness to be open to pain and suffering that we can allow the feeling of compassion to arise.

The practice of compassion means letting it all in: not defending against it, not avoiding it. Very often now in our society, we walk down the streets of many cities and confront the problem of homeless people. It is really a dreadful situation in our culture that there are people living on the streets. For me it is very interesting to watch my mind and ask, "How am I relating to these people?" What do we do, personally, as we pass by? It need not be any specific action, although many different actions could follow, but how do we relate? Are we letting this in? Are we really registering that this is the situation, that this is the suffering that is occurring? Or do we not want to let it in? Is it too unpleasant for us? Too distressing? Do we stay closed off?

In so many situations in our life, we face our spiritual practice right there. Letting it all in is the basis for compassion. Another Japanese poet, a woman named Izumi who lived in the tenth century, wrote: "Watching the moon at dawn. Solitary. Mid-sky. I knew myself completely. No part left out." That is our task: no part left out.

When we are open to all parts of ourselves and to all parts of other people in the world, something quite extraordinary happens. We actually begin to connect with one another. One of the most powerful experiences in my meditation practice occurred quite a few years ago. I was doing a Zen *sesshin* with Sasaki Roshi, a very fierce old Zen master. He expressed himself in a classic Zen mode, belligerent and demanding, and this was the first time I had done any Zen practice. The whole situation of the *sesshin* was geared to making you uptight. Roshi worked with the *koan* method. The *koan* is a problem the master gives you that does not have a rational answer. One of the most famous *koans* is "What is the sound of one hand clapping?" There are many other *koan* questions.

In this *sesshin* I saw Roshi four times a day to give him the answer to my *koan*. Everything in the *sesshin* is very structured, very tight, building the tension and the charge. I went in with my answers, but each time Roshi just rang his bell to dismiss me and said, "Oh, very stupid." This went on and on. Each time I would come in with my answer he would say, "Okay, but not Zen." It was totally demeaning, and I was getting more and more uptight. Finally, I think he had a little compassion for me, and he gave me an easier *koan*. He moved me back, I guess. He asked, "How do you manifest the Buddha while chanting a *sutra*?" I understood that the principle was to go in and chant a little of a *sutra* or discourse. We had been doing some *sutra* chanting every day.

I do not think Sasaki Roshi knew, although he might have known, that this *koan* plugged in exactly to some very deep conditioning in me going back to the third grade. Our singing teacher back then had said, "Goldstein, just mouth the words." From then on I have had a tremendous inhibition about singing, and now here I was, having to perform in a very charged situation. I was a total wreck. In the pressure cooker of the *sesshin*, which is held in silence except for the interviews, everything becomes magnified so much.

I rehearsed and rehearsed two lines of chant, all the while getting more and more tight, more and more tense. The bell rang for the interview, I went in, I started chanting, and I messed up the entire thing. I got all the words wrong; I felt completely exposed and vulnerable and raw. And Roshi just looked at me and with great feeling said, "Very good." It was a moment of heart touching heart, and it was powerful, because I saw that to receive compassion, to receive love, and to connect with both, takes a willingness to be open to one's vulnerability, a willingness to be exposed. That is when we can connect, heart to heart.

Clear Sky, Open Mind

So then, what is the wisdom that makes compassion possible? What do we need to understand in order to stay open to suffering? It is very simple and very profound: genuine happiness in our lives does not come from the accumulation of more and more pleasant feelings. If happiness actually depended on pleasant feelings, it would be a very limited kind of happiness, because pleasant feelings come and go. They do not last very long. Just think how many pleasant feelings you have had in your life. We have all had a countless number of pleasant, wonderful, ecstatic feelings. But we know when we reflect on our lives and on having experienced so many nice things and pleasant feelings, that somehow they have not provided lasting fulfillment. They have not created a place of lasting peace. We know that fact if we just stop to reflect a little bit.

If true happiness does not come from pleasant feelings, what does it come from? That question is at the heart of the practice of meditation. In meditation and, by extension, in our lives and in the world, it is not important what the particular experience is. What *is* important is how we relate to the experience. In some ways you can think of meditation as the art of relationship. When there is sorrow, anger, or fear, there is also a wide range of possible relationships. Are we caught in the experience? Do we identify with it? Is the mind spacious toward it? Is the mind observing it? By learning how to relate well to such things, we can actually come to a place of profound openness of mind.

You can think of the mind as a clear sky. All kinds of things pass through the sky, but the sky is not affected. It is possible to develop a mind like that, a mind that is not lost in or attached to phenomena. Such a mind experiences a much more abiding kind of happiness, because it does not depend on changing conditions. But our whole society and popular culture reinforce the belief that happiness comes primarily through pleasant feelings. One advertisement for cigarettes pictures a beautiful man and woman in paradise lounging with one another and with cigarettes, and the caption reads, "Nothing stands in the way of my pleasure." The message is: "Get this and you will be happy. Feel this and you will be happy."

The tremendous danger of such understanding is that if we believe genuine happiness comes only from pleasant feelings, we are motivated to stay closed to everything unpleasant. If we stay closed to what is unpleasant, we are also staying closed to our own wellspring of compassion. *Happiness does not depend on pleasant feelings.* We need to make that transformation of wisdom and understanding in ourselves. When we open to the full range of human experience, then we allow compassion to grow within us.

It is important to see compassion as a practice. Sometimes we feel it, sometimes we do not. Sometimes the suffering is too much, and we have to back off a little bit. We have to close off a little to prevent being overwhelmed. At such times we need to create a space where we can build some strength, and then, from that place of strength, we can open up to suffering again. Like lovingkindness, slowly we practice compassion, making it stronger.

Compassion does not manifest itself in any particular way. I think it is very problematic to make a hierarchy of compassionate actions. We all respond to suffering in different ways, based on our interests or skills, based on what moves us. But the whole world is a field for compassionate action, if we let in all the parts of ourselves and all the parts of the world. From that openness compassion flows.

The Dalai Lama goes to the heart of things in the most simple and down-to-earth way. He has said, "We are visitors on this planet. We are here for ninety, one hundred years at the most. During that period we must try to do something good, something useful with our lives. Try to be at peace with yourself, and help others to share that peace. If you contribute to other people's happiness, you will find the true goal, the true meaning in life."

It is very simple. We are here for a very short time. Can we try to do something good with our lives? Can we develop an inner peace and share that inner peace with others? If we contribute to other people's happiness, we find the true meaning, the true goal of life. This is our task. This is our challenge.

II

THE PRACTICE OF FREEDOM

*T*he question of living a spiritual life in the contemporary age has particular import, because in Buddhist cultures and traditions people who are deeply committed to a spiritual life and to spiritual awakening very commonly enter monasteries. This choice has been common in the Buddhist countries of Asia, where a tremendously powerful cultural value has been placed on having hundreds of thousands of monks and nuns and huge monasteries. Single monasteries in Tibet housed tens of thousands of monks or nuns.

As Buddhism has come to the west, it has not been particularly monastic. Rather, this tradition has been transmitted into a lay culture. The great question and challenge, for me in my teaching and for all of us involved with this transmission, is whether we can maintain in this different mode the highest spiritual values, the highest spiritual goals. Can we maintain a commitment to freedom, to awakening, and to enlightenment, in the midst of our modern culture? Or are we simply doing a spiritual practice in order to live a little more comfortably in our lives?

If we are committed to the highest goal of the spiritual life, it is essential that we have a very clear and precise sense of the path. If we are not clear about the path of spiritual practice in the complexity of our busy lives, it will become diluted. If we are aiming for the highest path, if this is what we value, then we need to be extremely clear and specific about what constitutes the spiritual life—not in theory, but in practice. How can we actually live it?

All the spiritual traditions share this underlying endeavor. One way of expressing it is to purify our minds and our hearts from the forces of greed, hatred, and delusion. That is not a particularly Buddhist idea. As forces in our minds, greed and hatred, delusion and ignorance, cause suffering in our own lives and in the world. There may be many techniques in many different spiritual traditions to accomplish this purification, but their common denominator, this process of purification, actually constitutes the genuine spiritual path. How can we transform ourselves, our minds, and our hearts, and free ourselves from the forces that create suffering?

The Buddha talked of three very simple trainings, three arenas of our life that are what the spiritual life is about. In the first training, the field of morality, we pay attention to our actions and speech and realize that what we do and say in our lives is very important. We cannot divorce spiritual practice from the everyday actions of our life. Morality is the principle of not harming. The Buddha spoke of morality as the true beauty of a person. Through it we commit ourselves not to harm ourselves or others. It is interesting to me that in our society, somehow the word "morality" has gotten a bad name. People associate it with righteousness or being moralistic. A whole range of connotations make us shy away from it. But the essence of morality is essential for the spiritual path.

In order to honor this commitment to morality, we pay attention to what we do. We wake up to our actions. If we take a moment to reflect on this aspect of our lives, we see that there are different ways we can train ourselves. For example, we can watch the effect of our actions on our own minds. When we do something, how does it affect us? How do we feel? What qualities do our actions strengthen? Every time we get angry, we practice anger. Every time we are filled with resentment, we practice resentment. The more we do them, the stronger those qualities grow. Every time we feel loving or perform some loving, generous act, that is what we practice. So it becomes clear that <u>every action in our lives is our practice</u>, because there is actually some quality of heart and mind being strengthened. <u>We need to look at and pay attention to very ordinary activities</u>. When we talk with people, what is the quality of our minds? What is our motive? When we eat or work, what is the quality of our minds? This is the "juice" of moral training—really becoming awake to what we are doing.

We can pay attention not only to how our actions affect us and what we are developing and strengthening, but we can also pay attention to how our actions affect other people. Can we be sensitive to the effect of our energy on others in the different acts we perform? Often we are so caught up in our own story that we do not pay careful attention to the impact we are having. Training in morality, training in not harming, means that we develop a sensitivity. We begin to look at the motives behind our actions and speech. This is very subtle, and there is tremendous room here for self-delusion. We can think we are acting with great nobility, and yet, when we look honestly and deeply and carefully, we may see otherwise.

Here is a simple example. Years ago I was

30

practicing meditation in India. Anybody who spends any time at all in India must come to terms with the countless number of people begging. It is just part of reality there, and one is in relationship to it one way or another. I was in the bazaar one day buying some fruit. There were a lot of beggars around, and one little boy was holding out his hand. He looked hungry, so I took one of the oranges I had bought and gave it to him. It felt good to respond to him. But he just took the orange and walked away. Not a smile, not a nod, not a thank-you, nothing. Only when he did that, only in the absence of a response, did I see clearly that some part of my mind, some part of my generosity, some part of my motive had wanted an acknowledgment. I had not been expecting effusive thanks for the orange, but I had wanted something. And this child just took the orange and walked away.

The relationship between our motives and our quality of mind is very subtle. Can we give truly without any expectation of getting something back, just for the joy of giving? Becoming very honest with ourselves is part of our training in morality. It takes a tremendous awareness, and we need to look at ourselves very carefully.

How do we practice this kind of training? How do we actually do it? So often we hear these ideas and say, "Yes, that's a good idea. It is good not to harm." We may even coast on the understanding that we are basically moral people. We are not going around killing people or stealing or doing various harmful things. The real awakening comes when we see that we can greatly refine our morality. It comes with training; it is not a given. When we understand this—from whatever place we're starting, from whatever our degree of commitment to non-harming—our moral sense can become increasingly refined. That is what makes the practice of morality so powerful.

All religious traditions express the basic moral precepts in different ways, but they also have much in common. In traditional Buddhism laypeople practice the five precepts: not killing, not stealing, not committing sexual misconduct, not using wrong speech, and not taking intoxicants that confuse the mind. These guidelines are very simple, very basic. But each one of these precepts is also a practice.

Some time ago I was getting a haircut in a barber shop. There was a fly buzzing around, so the barber grabbed his fly swatter and killed the fly. "Do not kill it," I thought as I sat in the chair. From an ordinary, worldly perspective, killing a fly is nothing; people do it all the time. From another, moral perspective, however, we do not need to go around killing the flies. We can connect with the life that is in that fly. There are other ways of dealing with the fly.

I have spent many hours catching insects in a cup and taking them outside. We can do that. We can change our relationship to other living creatures. This is not to suggest that the answers are always clear-cut and easy. If termites are eating up your house, what do you do? Do you say, "Be happy, be happy"? Or do you call the exterminator? Ethical decisions are not always easy. But we can become committed to training ourselves to look for alternatives to killing. We can practice not killing, and can take that practice further than we have.

We can also practice morality in speech, a large area of our lives. How much of the day do we spend talking? Huge amounts. Speech is a powerful force. But how much attention do we pay to our speech? I think for most people care in this area of life is rare. We are caught up in what we have to say, and we say it. Do we actually bring some wisdom and sensitivity to our speaking? What is behind our speech, what motivates it? Does something really have to be said?

When I was first getting into the practice of thinking and learning about speech, I conducted an experiment. For several months I decided not to speak about any third person; I would not speak to somebody about somebody else. No gossip. Ninety percent of my speech was eliminated. Before I did that, I had no idea that I had spent so much time and energy engaged in that kind of talking. It is not that my speech had been particularly malicious, but for the most part it had been useless. I found it tremendously interesting to watch the impact this experiment had on my mind. As I stopped speaking in this way, I found that one way or another a lot of my speech had been a judgment about somebody else. By stopping such speech for a while, my mind became less judgmental, not only of others, but also of myself, and it was a great relief.

These are little things that have significant impact in our lives—how we live, how we feel. This is what morality is about. It is not something abstract. It is something to train ourselves in: no killing, no wrong speech, no sexual misconduct. These considerations are all very important, especially in our society now, where many traditional values are no longer in place. We need to take a lot of care. Under the power of desire and passion, very strong forces, people do many things that may not be "skillful"—things that may actually cause harm to themselves and to other people. We need to look, to pay attention.

There are many more examples. Training in morality is a practice, and it is the foundation of a spiritual life. One of my first teachers visited America and met people interested in meditation, but not so committed to the practice of moral training. He said people who want great spiritual insight without actually grounding the meditation in moral action, are like somebody in a rowboat putting tremendous effort and exertion into rowing across a river, while not untying the boat from the dock: nothing happens. We can put all kinds of effort into many kinds of meditative and spiritual techniques. But if we are not committed to the groundwork of morality—and this does not mean being moralistic or self-righteous—then we do not actually progress in the spiritual life. It requires paying attention to our actions and being committed to doing no harm. This takes a lot of honesty, so that we do not fool ourselves.

There is a wonderful American monk, Ajahn Sumedo, who trained for years in Thailand. He is the chief western disciple of one of the great Thai meditation masters, and now he has several monasteries in England. He has said with great succinctness that our practice is not to follow the heart; it is to *train* the heart. Here is a tremendously important distinction. I do not know about you, but as I have sat and practiced and looked at the different things that have come up in my heart, some have been fine, beautiful, noble. But many things that have come out of this heart have not been so noble. The heart can be driven by desire, greed, and anger. We need to train the heart, not simply to follow it.

This commitment to morality, to not harming, is a source of tremendous strength, precisely because there is no remorse in the heart. It gives us the ability to die without confusion. We die with clarity. Non-harming is the great gift of fearlessness, and not just for ourselves. When we commit to not harming, with our actions we are saying to everyone we meet, "You do not need to fear me." In this world, that is a very precious gift. We are giving the gift of trust to people. We have all acted unskillfully in the past, but the strength and power of morality begin from the moment we commit ourselves to skillful action. It is not that we will always be totally pure; that is unrealistic. But we do need to have started. Imagine what life on this planet would be like if people followed just one precept: no killing. The world would be transformed, a different place.

This heart-training is what we can do if we are committed to awakening, and it is essential that we do it. It has a tremendous impact on our spiritual lives because a morality of doing no harm frees our minds from remorse. Freedom from remorse leads to happiness. Happiness leads to concentration. Concentration brings wisdom. And wisdom is the source of happiness, beauty, and freedom in our lives.

The Buddha taught that morality is the true beauty of a human being, not one's physical appearance or outer adornments. I think we all recognize this to be true when we are with people who are living from that place of basic goodness within themselves. By refining our own practice of morality, non-harming, we reteach ourselves our loveliness. The New England poet Galway Kinnell wrote in "Saint Francis and the Sow":

The bud
stands for all things,
even for those things that don't flower,
for everything flowers, from within, of self-blessing;
though sometimes it is necessary
to reteach a thing its loveliness,
to put a hand on its brow
of the flower
and retell it in words and in touch
it is lovely
until it flowers again from within, of self-blessing;

So the practice of morality, non-harming, is the first field of training, and it requires developing and refining very specific practices.

The second field of training has to do with the development of concentration and a very strong, mindful awareness. Without strong and concentrated mindfulness, we cannot see clearly. We do not know exactly what is going on.

Those who meditate know very well that the mind is often scattered. In meditation we give the mind a simple object: Feel the breath, watch the breath. But what happens? We feel it, we observe one breath, two breaths, and then the mind goes off. It becomes lost in thoughts and memories and plans and judgments, in our likes and dislikes. We hop on a train of associations, unaware that we have done so. We do not even know where the train is going. And then somewhere down the track we wake up and think, "Oh, look where I have gotten to!" This is the common condition of our scattered, slippery minds. Sometimes it reminds me of being in a movie theater where the film changes every couple of minutes. Our minds are like that. We would not stay in a movie theater if that were happening, but what can we do about this nonstop internal screening?

We need to train ourselves to concentrate, to get focused, to stay more steadily with each breath. We begin to see that the mind can be trained. It is slow, and it takes time, but an inner stillness is possible.

When I first started meditation practice, I thought all the time. There was no concentration at all. I would sit down and think for the hour. Then I would get up and say, "That was a nice sitting." It took a lot of time and a lot of perseverance for my mind to settle down. As we meditate, we bring our attention back to the object, and at the same time we become more accepting and a little more "spacious" toward what is going on. Then an amazing thing happens: We find that we are less driven, in the meditation and in our lives, either by the force of denial or by the force of addiction. Much of life is driven by these two forces—denial and addiction. In the meditative process we become quieter, more still, more spacious, more accepting; we are more willing to see whatever is there. We are with it, but we are not caught by it. We let go.

What happens when we do not let go? Asians have a very clever trap for catching monkeys. People hollow out a coconut, put something sweet in it, and make a hole in the bottom of the coconut just big enough for the monkey to slide its open hand in, but not big enough for the monkey to withdraw its hand as a fist. They attach the coconut to a tree, and the monkey comes along and gets trapped. What keeps the monkey trapped? Only the force of desire, of clinging, of attachment. All the monkey has to do is let go of the sweet, open its hand, slip it out, and be free. But only a very rare monkey will do that.

With meditation we also begin to develop a sense of humor. Humor is essential on the spiritual path, and it is inevitable. If you do not have a sense of humor now, meditate for awhile and it will come, because it is impossible to watch this bizarre mind steadily and systematically without learning how to smile. Someone once asked Sasaki Roshi whether he went to the movies. "No," he replied. "I give interviews."

Some years ago I was on retreat with my teacher, U Pandita Sayadaw, a Burmese monk and meditation master. He is a strict teacher, so everyone in the retreat was being very quiet, impeccable, mindful. Everyone moved very slowly. It was an intense time of training. In silence the whole retreat entered the dining room and began taking food, very mindfully. I was second in line for food one day. The first person went through the line, lifted up the cover on a pot of food, and put it down on the table. It dropped to the floor and made a huge racket. Everything had been totally still and quiet, and then came this huge noise. The first thought in my mind was, "It wasn't me." Now, where did that thought come from?

"The mind has no pride," someone told me once. Through the practice of meditation, one begins to see this truth, one of the insights of insight meditation. The mind will put out anything, and it does. We can learn to be with that passing show. We can learn to be accepting, to possess a certain lightness and sense of humor about it all. The lighter and more accepting we are with ourselves, the lighter and more accepting we are with other people. We are not so prone to judge the minds of others once we have seen our own minds.

It is essential to develop a concentrated mind. There is no way to open ourselves to deeper levels of experience without practicing and training ourselves to concentrate, to stay focused, to stay open. Without this power of concentration, we stay on the surface of things. If we are committed to higher spiritual values, we need to practice concentration, not simply to talk about it. We can develop our concentration. We can do it for ourselves, each one of us.

I began to practice meditation when I was in the Peace Corps in Thailand. At that time I was very enthusiastic about philosophy and debating, and when I first went to visit Buddhist monks, I arrived with a copy of Spinoza in my hand in order to debate them. I started going to discussion groups led by some western monks.

But I was so persistent in my questions that other people stopped coming. Finally, out of desperation one of the poor monks said, "Listen, why don't you start meditating?" I think they just needed to get me quiet.

I did not know anything about meditation at the time, and I became very excited by it. I gathered all the paraphernalia together, sat myself down on a cushion, and set my alarm clock for five minutes (I did not want to oversit). But something very important happened even in those first five minutes. I realized that I could do it. That realization is a turning point in everyone's spiritual life. We read books and hear people speak about it, but then we reach a certain point in our lives when something connects and we realize, "Yes, I can do this." This does not mean that in those first five minutes I reached any great state of awakening; I did not. But I saw very clearly that there is a way to look inward. There is a path. There is a way to explore the nature of the mind, the nature of our lives.

This was the very first step. It was so new and interesting to me that for a while I used to invite my friends over to watch me meditate. They didn't often come back. I am still doing it, but I just call it something else. Now I say, "Come to a retreat."

Practicing in Daily Life

In our busy lives and our complex and confusing culture, how can we develop concentration? The first thing is to become committed to a daily, regular discipline of practice. We need to train ourselves to do it regularly. Discipline is not just going to drop down from heaven. It is going to come through our own efforts. There are many meditation techniques and traditions, and you can find the one that is most suitable for you. But it is the regularity of the practice that begins to effect a transformation. If we do it, it begins to happen. If we do not do it, it does not happen.

The second step in this practice is training ourselves to stay in the body, to stay mindful and aware of the body throughout the day. Most of the time we go through the day, through our activities, our work, our relationships, our conversations, and very rarely do we ground ourselves in an awareness of our bodies. We are lost in our thoughts, our feelings, our emotions, our stories, our plans.

A very simple guide or check on this state of being lost is to pay attention to those times when you feel like you are rushing. Rushing does not have to do with speed. You can rush moving slowly, and you can rush moving quickly. We are rushing when we feel as if we are toppling forward. Our minds run ahead of ourselves; they are out there where we want to get to, instead of being settled back in our bodies. The feeling of rushing is good feedback. Whenever we are not present, right then, in that situation, we should stop and take a few deep breaths. Settle into the body again. Feel yourself sitting. Feel the step of a walk. Be in your body.

The Buddha made a very powerful statement about this: "Mindfulness of the body leads to nirvana." Such awareness is not a superficial practice. Mindfulness of the body keeps us present. We know what is happening. This practice is difficult to remember, but not difficult to do. It is all in the training: sitting regularly; practicing daily; staying mindful of the body; being aware of thoughts and emotions.

Have you ever stopped to consider what a thought is? Very few people really stop to ask, "What is a thought?" But doing so is tremendously important, because when we are not aware of our thoughts, and we are not aware of the nature of thoughts, they absolutely drive and dominate our lives. Thoughts drive us, they pull us, as if we were slaves to them. Thoughts tell us to do this, say that, go here, go there.

Years ago when I was teaching in Boulder, Colorado, I was sitting quite comfortably in my apartment. Thoughts were coming and going. I thought, "Oh, a pizza would be nice." The thought lifted me up. It took me out the door and through all the hassles of going to get the pizza and then burning my mouth because I ate too quickly. What drove that whole sequence? Just a thought in my mind.

Obviously, there is nothing wrong with going to get a pizza; but what merits our attention is how much our lives are driven by thoughts. Unnoticed, they have great power. And yet when we have enough attention, enough mindfulness actually to observe thoughts arising in the mind, we can sit back, see thoughts emerge in the mind and pass away, and realize that when we notice them, thoughts seem totally empty of substance. It is like the Wizard of Oz: there is no one behind the curtain. But we do not always see that simple truth.

To see the empty nature of thoughts frees us tremendously. They feel like little bubbles in the mind, and from that perspective it does not matter what the thoughts are saying. All thoughts come and go, and then we have some space to choose among them. We have the freedom and the space to say, "Yes, I will act on this one; I won't act on that one." So we pay attention. We really learn to see thoughts instead of simply being lost in them.

We also train ourselves to do the same with

emotions, which are also powerful forces in our lives. Anger, sadness, sorrow, grief, love, compassion, envy, and jealousy—every day we experience a huge range of emotions. There are beautiful ones and difficult ones, and most of the time we are totally caught up in their story. We are lost in our own melodrama.

It is very interesting to drop down a level and look at the energy of the emotion. What is sadness? What is anger? Seeing more deeply in this way requires looking not at the story behind the emotion, but rather looking at how the emotion works in our lives and in our minds. It means really taking an interest in discovery, rather than drowning in the story of it all. To do it takes mindfulness, attention, and concentration.

I am not suggesting that we should not allow emotions to come, or that we should push them aside. I am suggesting instead a complete openness to feelings when they arise. How do we relate to an emotion? What is the quality of mind that holds it? We can be completely identified with an emotion, or we can have a spaciousness of mind that feels the grief, the rage, the sadness, the joy. The feeling is still complete, but we experience it without a sense of identification. Taking that emotion to be me or mine is the spiritual knot; that is where we limit ourselves and contract into a small self.

One monk from Sri Lanka used to say, "No self, no problem." Can we begin to understand even a little of what this means? We can, through a daily practice, a daily discipline that trains us to be in the body, to pay attention to thoughts and emotions. All of these are ways of training ourselves and our minds to concentrate.

To develop deeper concentration and mindfulness, to be more present in our bodies, and to see our right relationship to thoughts and emotions, we need not only a daily training, but also some time for retreat. This is essential. We need to withdraw from the busyness of our lives for some intensive spiritual practice. Retreat is not a luxury. If we are genuinely, sincerely, and deeply committed to awakening, to freedom, to whatever word expresses the highest value we hold, it is absolutely essential. We need to create a rhythm in our lives, to establish a balance between the times when we are engaged and active and relating, and the times when we turn inward.

Should we be surprised at the confused state of the world? People do not take the time to quiet down; they do not see the importance or the value of going inside themselves. At first this going inside could be for a day. It could be for a weekend; it could be for ten days. At our meditation center we offer a three-month retreat every year. In the Tibetan tradition there are three-year retreats. Do whatever feels appropriate to get into some balanced rhythm, to take time for retreat, to go inward, to be out of the world. By doing this you can develop concentration, mindfulness, and awareness on deeper and deeper levels, which makes possible being back in the world in a more loving and compassionate way.

To sum up: The first field of training is morality and inner beauty. The second is concentration and mindful awareness. The third is wisdom. How do we cultivate wisdom in our lives? Through specific meditative practice, and also through wise attention in our lives. Just by paying attention, tremendous wisdom becomes available to us.

The Light of Wisdom

Times of difficulty in our lives present us with one rich, but commonly overlooked, source of wisdom. When we are going through some period of suffering, we can learn so much about the nature of suffering and the nature of freedom, but only if we are sufficiently motivated to look carefully at the situation. Often in times of difficulty people tend only to look outward with blame or judgment. Sometimes we might also look inward with self blame and self judgment.

Instead, we should let go of the judgments and take interest in the suffering itself. What is causing it? What are the forces at work in our minds? Is there attachment, possessiveness, fear, expectation? We need to see what is really going on.

We develop wisdom through very clear seeing and recollection of impermanence, and through the recollection of death. This is a powerful teaching. We can see impermanence on so many levels, from the rising and passing away of clusters of galaxies to the impermanence of moments in the human mind. Reflection on impermanence leads us to one very important and demanding question. When we experience the truth of impermanence, not just as a concept, but as a genuinely felt insight, we are forced to ask, "What is truly of value?" Are we valuing something that is simply going to pass away? Or is there something else, something greater?

It helps me to imagine myself on my deathbed. I feel myself dying, and I look back. I think about what I would have wanted to accomplish in my life. This reflection provides a powerful perspective. The secret is to ask the question now before our deaths, with a clear sense of vision. It clarifies our sense of purpose and vision for our lives. Then we can make the appropriate choices, because we see what is of value and then do it. Otherwise, it is as if life unfolds and there is not much direction to it; we are buffeted by circumstances. And then one day it is over. We do not need to live and die that way, but in order not to, we need to be clear about our values and about what human greatness can be accomplished.

Wisdom comes from a deep understanding of impermanence. It also develops through a greater and greater experience of selflessness, of moving beyond our very small world of ego identification. There is a momentous difference between being lost in or identified with a thought, and the spaciousness of mind that simply sees the thought rise and pass away. The first is a prison; the second is like a vast, open sky. Thoughts that wander through our minds have no roots, no home. But we root them. For every thought that comes through our minds we say, "This is mine. This is who I am." And so we feel constricted and contracted in our lives.

Wisdom can move us beyond that sense of contraction and self-identification, just as the light of a single candle can dispel the darkness of a thousand years. No matter how long or deep our confusion, in the moment of lighting a single candle of wisdom and attention, for that moment ignorance is dispelled.

This is our practice: to refine our morality by paying attention to our actions, to concentrate,

50

to be mindful, to develop and deepen all of these practices so that the candle of wisdom can indeed illuminate our lives. These teachings and practices present themselves to us in the spirit of an invitation to come and see, to take a look at our lives and to see for ourselves. That is the real nature of the spiritual journey.